JOAN TOWER

IVORY AND EBONY

FOR PIANO

AMP 8317
First Printing: July 2017

ISBN: 978-1-4950-9567-2

Associated Music Publishers, Inc.

DISTRIBUTED BY

HAL•LEONARD®
www.halleonard.com
www.musicsalesclassical.com

Commissioned by the San Antonio International Piano Competition
in Memory of Andrew Russell Gurwitz

First performed on October 17, 2009
by the San Antonio International Piano Competition contestants
San Antonio, TX

Composer Note:

Ivory and Ebony was written for the 2009 San Antonio International Piano Competition. The "themes" in the work are based on the black and white notes of the piano, often played separately but occasionally together at climactic points. This composition was designed as a virtuoso piece for the outstanding piano competitors of the competition.

— Joan Tower

IVORY AND EBONY has been recorded
by Blair McMillen for future release on Naxos Records
www.naxos.com

duration circa 8 minutes

Information on Joan Tower and her works is available on musicsalesclassical.com

for my friend and colleague Blair McMillen

IVORY AND EBONY

Joan Tower

* In bars 50–52, the right hand starts shortly after the left. The rhythm shown is not precise.

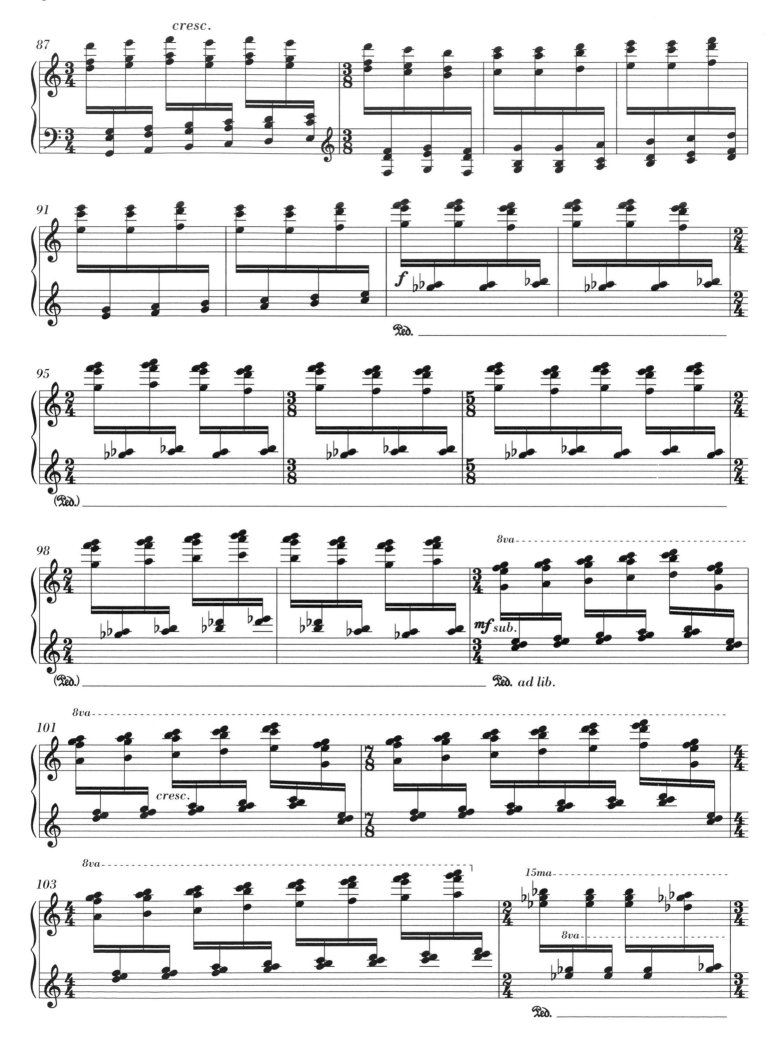

* In bars 154–156, the right hand rhythms are approximate. Try to avoid playing with the hands together.

* In bars 166–178, the right hand rhythms are approximate. Try to avoid playing with the hands together.

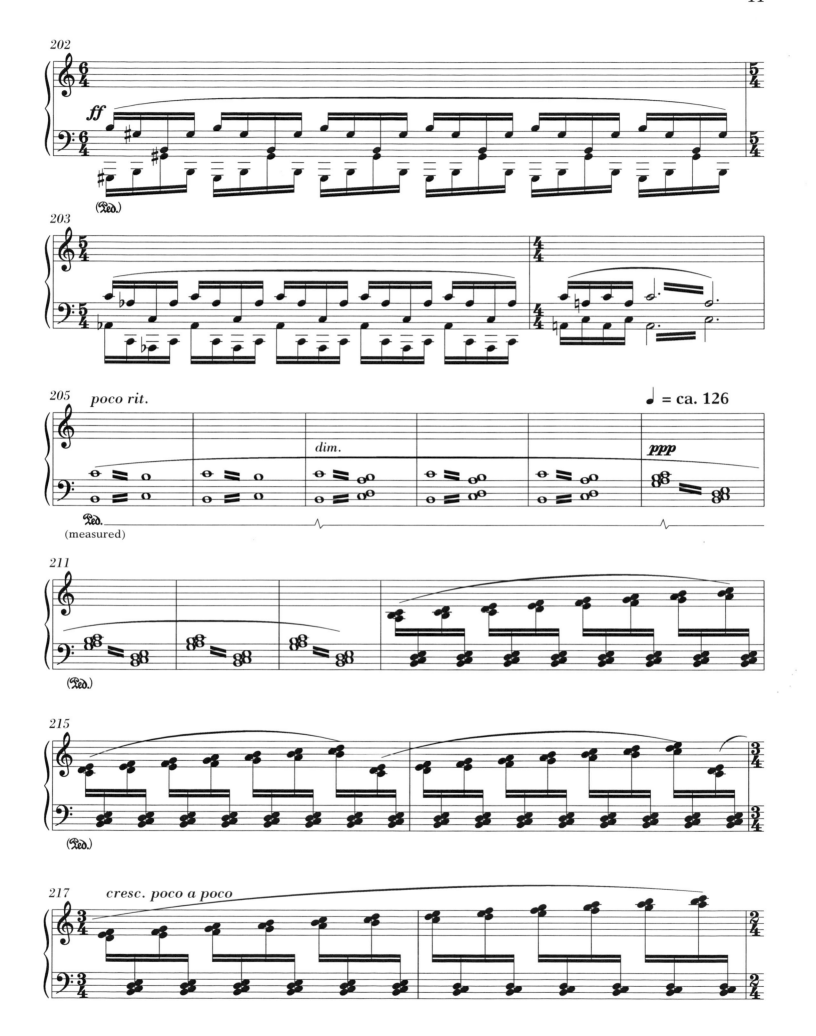

* Overlap *glisses* slightly so they flow without break.